50¢

Drawing
o
People

Barbara Soloff Levy

Dover Publications, Inc.
Mineola, New York

Bibliographical Note

Drawing on the Go! People, first published by Dover
Publications, Inc., in 2012, is a republication in a different format
of the work originally published as *How to Draw People* by Dover
Publications, Inc., in 2002.

International Standard Book Number

ISBN-13: 978-0-486-48882-0
ISBN-10: 0-486-48882-9

Manufactured in the United States by Courier Corporation
48882905   2014
www.doverpublications.com

Note

It's so easy to draw people, and this handy little book will show you how! Using just a few steps, you will create pictures of a schoolgirl, a roller skater, a boy on a swing, and much more. You'll start with a simple shape and then add more details. You may want to trace the steps for each picture first, and then you can begin to draw using a pencil, which is easy to erase. Follow the steps in number order. Erase and draw new lines until you are happy with your picture. You can use colored pencils or felt-tip pens to finish your work. Finally, you can color your picture to make the people come to life!

2 Baby boy

Practice Page

4 Baby girl

Practice Page

6 Boy

Practice Page

8 Girl with doll

Practice Page

10 Schoolgirl

Practice Page

12 Baseball player

Practice Page

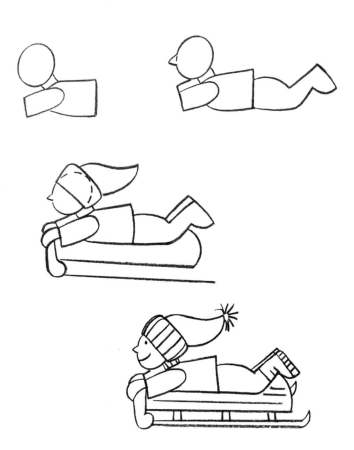

14 Child on sled

Practice Page

16 Roller skater

Practice Page

18 Boy on swing

Practice Page

20 Girl with fishing rod

Practice Page

22 Boy with toy train

Practice Page

24 Child with kite

Practice Page

26 Hockey player

Practice Page

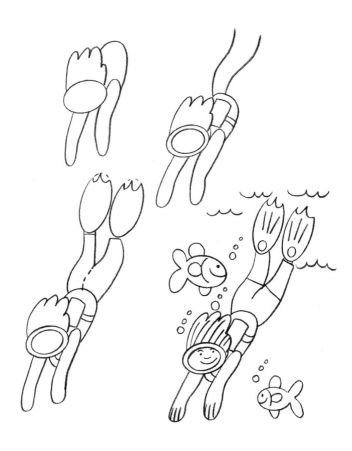

28 Scuba diver

Practice Page

30 Tennis player

Practice Page

32 Skateboarder

Practice Page

34 Softball player

Practice Page

36 Boy with beach ball

Practice Page

38 Marching band drummer

Practice Page

40 Hiker

Practice Page

42 Businessman

Practice Page

44 Postal worker

Practice Page

46 Ice cream man

Practice Page

48 Woman with cake

Practice Page

50 Astronaut

Practice Page

52 Firefighter

Practice Page

54 Cowboy

Practice Page

56 Painter

Practice Page

58 Dancer

Practice Page

60 Faces

Practice Page